Anita Ganeri

Illustrated by Steve Cox

Hippo

Scholastic Children's Books,
Commonwealth House, 1-19 New Oxford Street,
London WC1A 1NU, UK
a division of Scholastic Ltd
London ~ New York ~ Toronto ~ Sydney ~ Auckland

First published in the UK by Scholastic Ltd, 1997

ISBN 0 590 13149 4

Printed and bound in Spain by G.Z. Printek

10 9 8 7 6 5 4 3 2 1

In most respects, Rebecca Trekker, commonly known as "Boots", and her younger brother, Tim, commonly known as Tim, were two quite ordinary children. They lived in a quite ordinary house and they went to a quite ordinary school.

Their family was quite ordinary, too. Except for batty Aunt Agatha. Aunt Agatha was the green sheep of the family. A celebrated scientist and keen environmentalist, she was constantly on the move, travelling the world in search of rare and endangered plants and animals.

Aunt Agatha had just set off on another of her expeditions. Unfortunately, she had forgotten to tell anyone where she was going.

I wonder where A.A. is now?

No sooner had Boots uttered these words…

…than a postman arrived with a parcel. It was covered in lots of exotic stamps and had a label which read:

TO REBECCA AND TIM TREKKER, PRIVATE AND PERSONAL

Boots and Tim tore open the parcel excitedly.

Inside was one of Aunt Agatha's famous travel diaries and a carefully folded map. A tape cassette fell out of the map, together with a lot of sand.

Brilliant! My tape recorder's chewed up Aunt Agatha's tape.

Don't worry, I think I can work out what the message says.

IN I'M SAHARA THE IN DESERT AFRICA NORTH (MAP SEE) I'VE AND MADE JUST AMAZING AN BRING DISCOVERY CAMERA MY AND IMMEDIATELY WILL ALL REVEALED BE STAYING I'M AN IN VILLAGE OASIS (X SEE MAP ON) AUNT LOVE P.S. AGATHA YOU IF ACROSS COME OF ANY HEART THOSE SWEETS SHAPED LIKE I BRING PLEASE PACKET A.

Can you work out what the message says?

4

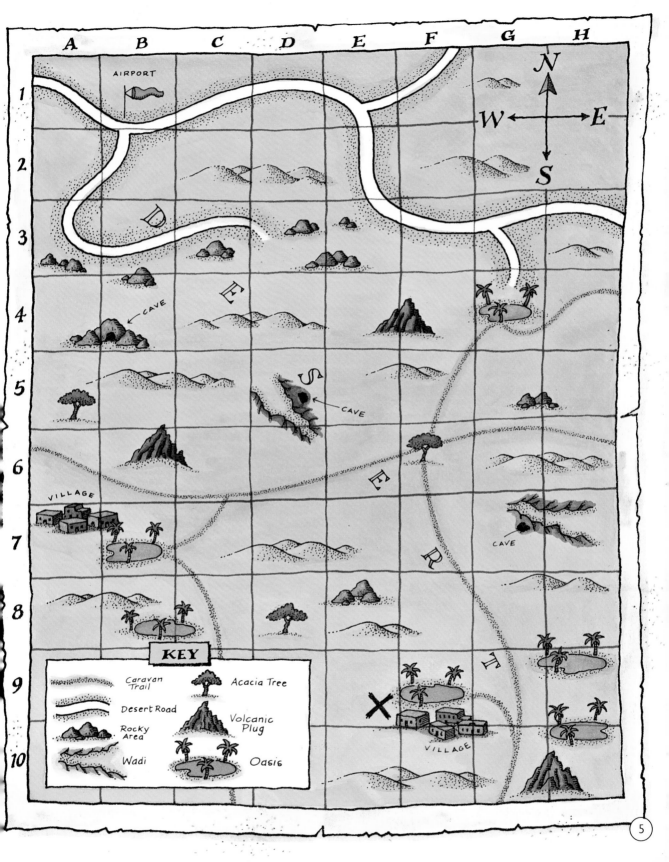

While Boots rushed around organizing their trip, Tim stuck his nose firmly in Aunt Agatha's travel diary. It was just the sort of book he liked, crammed with all sorts of notes and sketches, plus useful tips about how to survive in the desert. Tim and his sister were soon to find out just how tricky desert survival could be!

Let's see what Aunt Agatha's got to say about the Sahara.

DESERT DIARY

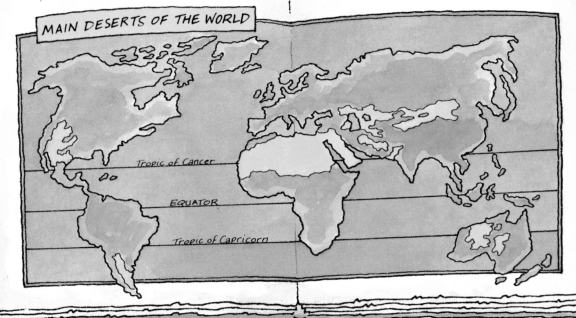

SURVIVAL GUIDE

Desert — a very hot, very dry place which typically receives less than 25cm of rain a year. Sometimes has no rain for years, then a sudden downpour and flash floods. Sometimes sandy, though not always — some are stony, rocky, gravelly, even volcanic. The biggest desert is the Sahara which covers 9 million square kilometres — a third of Africa. (That's big! A.A.)

MAIN DESERTS OF THE WORLD

Tropic of Cancer

EQUATOR

Tropic of Capricorn

Sand — if it's sand you want, the Sahara's the place for you. There's nothing but sand for miles and miles. Sand is made of tiny bits of crushed rock. (Murder on your teeth if it gets into your sandwiches! A.A.)

WARNING!!

Because of the lack of rainclouds, the Sahara is scorching hot by day. But don't be fooled! With no clouds to trap the heat, temperatures plummet to freezing by night. So wrap up warm.

DESERT DOS AND DON'TS — AT A GLANCE
DOS

DO drink plenty of water to fend off heatstroke and dehydration. But sip, DON'T guzzle it down.

DO stay cool. Rushing about will only make you sweat and lose precious water and salt.

DO wear sunglasses. The desert sun is very bright and will hurt your eyes.

DO wrap your scarf around your mouth and nose (not too tightly) to keep out sand and dust.

DO travel at night or in the early morning when it's cooler (if possible).

DON'TS

DON'T camp near a dry river valley (wadi). One flash flood and you'll be swept away. Best to sleep in a cave, if you can find one. (Caves are warmer and less exposed than sleeping out in the open.)

DON'T mess with desert snakes or scorpions. One false move could prove very painful.

DON'T forget to cover yourself with plenty of good, strong suncream. The desert sun is very hot.

DON'T do anything that might offend the locals. You never know when you might need them.

With Aunt Agatha's desert dos and don'ts ringing in their ears, Boots and Tim set off for the airport. On the way, they stopped off to collect some equipment for their trip.

I hope they've got everything we need.

Come on, we've got a plane to catch!

DRESSED FOR THE DESERT

1 shirt (loose, long-sleeved, cotton for coolness)

1 pair trousers (long, loose, cotton)

1 pair boots (sturdy)

1 pair socks (cotton)

1 hat (essential, wide-brimmed is best)

1 large hanky or scarf (for covering face and neck)

1 pair sunglasses

NB Travel light — you don't want to be lugging heavy rucksacks around in this heat.

ESSENTIAL SURVIVAL KIT

penknife
clean hankies (for head covers)
salt tablets (to replace salt lost through dehydration)
suncream (strong, plenty of it)
rucksack (lined with plastic to keep sand out)
compass
snakebite kit
mirror (for signalling in an emergency)
water bottle (or two, plastic)
torch
cup, plate, spoon
sleeping bag (it's cold at night)
matches
black plastic bin bag
(more useful than you think!)
Optional extras: blow up cushions and spares (for camel rides!). Items to barter with/give as gifts: sugar cubes, vitamin pills and flip flops.

Their packing problem sorted, Boots and Tim were soon on their way to North Africa.

We're just in time!

Well, here we go!

Now we've changed, let's go!

The jeep took them to the edge of the desert, then they were on their own.

I've found our position on Aunt Agatha's map. Now we need to head south through the desert to find the oasis she's marked.

I don't mean to be difficult, but which way's south?

How do Boots and Tim orientate their map?

Pretty soon they found south and set off. As they walked, Tim read up on the spectacular sandscape they were entering.

Deserts are very windy places. The wind piles the sand up into heaps (sand-dunes) or blasts it at the rocks and carves them into extraordinary shapes.

Volcanic plugs
These are volcanic rocks made from lava which cooled inside the pipes of volcanoes. The volcanoes are now extinct and have been worn away — but these plugs of lava can still be seen.

Sand roses
These fascinating rock formations can be found just below the surface of sand-dunes. They are made when dew dissolves gypsum in sand. The gypsum crystals join together to make sand-coloured disc shapes.

Fossils
Many parts of the Sahara were once beneath sea level (unbelievable, eh?) and embedded in rocks today are fossilized coral reefs, molluscs and snail shells.

Hammada
The heat of the Sahara turns these rocks black and makes them extremely hard. Even so, bacteria and lichen manage to live on these rocks and can even break them up into smaller pieces.

Sand-dunes
Different shapes depending on direction of wind. The biggest sand-dunes in the Sahara can be 40 times higher than a house! Sand-dunes move as sand trickles over the top and down the other side. (I've seen whole villages buried by sand. Not a pretty sight. AA.)

Once they'd got through the sand-dunes, Tim climbed to the top of one to get his bearings. But it was getting dark and he began to lose his footing...

This is no time to mess around, Tim!

Uh-oh!

Heeelp!

When Tim finally stopped rolling, he checked himself for damage. He was OK – but night was falling ... and fast.

NAVIGATING BY NIGHT, OR NEARLY NIGHT

1. Find the group of stars called the Big Dipper. (I call it the Giant Saucepan myself, A.A.)

2. Trace a line through the two stars at the end of the pan. The line will point at the North Star which shines above the North Pole.

3. If you want to go north, follow that star NB In different parts of the world, the Big Dipper looks like it's in a different position. In the Sahara, it's upside down!

I think the compass has got sand in it!

Can you spot the North Star?

12

Luckily, the compass wasn't broken. Turning their backs on the North Star, Boots and Tim continued their journey south.

Where are we? And more importantly, when can we stop? I'm whacked!

Whereabouts on the map are Boots and Tim now? Is there somewhere safe to sleep nearby?

By the time our two tired trekkers had found a suitable campsite, Boots was half asleep. While she slept, Tim lit a fire, to keep warm and to keep unwelcome desert animals at bay. Then he snuggled down into his sleeping bag, and read by the light of the fire.

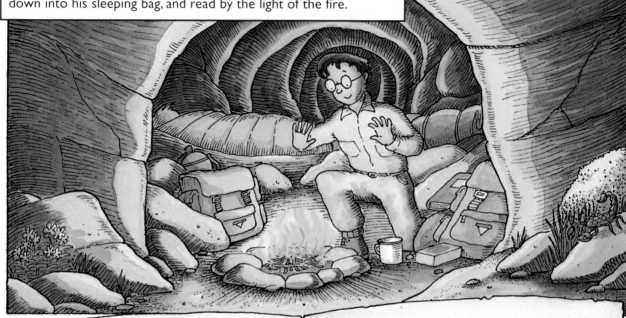

The desert may look bare and barren but an amazing number of animals survive the harsh conditions. They're not always easy to find. Many spend the day underground, where the sand is cooler. Others are camouflaged to look like the colour of sand.

Horned viper — a cunning creature this. Lies under the sand with just its eyes and horns showing and waits for a tasty snack to potter past. (NB Watch your step. This tasty snack could be your foot! Many desert snakes are EXTREMELY poisonous! AA) Nocturnal.

Jerboa — back legs four times as long as its front legs. Can hop like a champion to escape from enemies. Long tail to keep its balance. Nocturnal.

Fennec fox — has huge ears which give off excess heat and keep it cool. Handy for hearing too. Hunts jerboas at night.

Desert hedgehog — long legs for lifting its body above the hot sand. Spends the day in its burrow and hunts at night. Likes to lunch on desert scorpion (after first biting off its stinging tail).

Skink — sometimes called a sand fish because of its amazing ability to "swim" through sand. It does this to keep cool during the day ... and to keep hidden from hungry enemies.

Sand cat — nocturnal creature. Has fur on its feet to protect them from the heat of the ground and stop it sinking into the sand. (With feet like that, who needs slippers? AA)

Later that night, a sneaky desert creature crept into the cave and rummaged through our travellers' belongings.

Do you know which animal is the intruder? What disaster awaits Boots and Tim when they wake up?

Early the next morning, Boots woke up with a raging thirst ... only to discover that her water bottle was empty.

Aaaargh!

Fresh supplies had to be found ... and fast. Once again, Aunt Agatha's diary came up trumps.

But where are we going to find plastic in the desert?

To collect water, simply make a solar still.
1. Dig a hole in the ground.
2. Put a cup in the middle of the hole.
3. Cover the hole with a plastic sheet and put a stone in the middle to weigh the plastic down over the cup while the edges are held down with other stones.
4. Wait for the water in the ground to condense on to the plastic and drip into the cup.

Start early! It'll take about a day to collect three cups of water. (AA.)

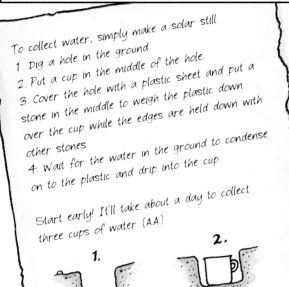

Which piece of their desert equipment has Tim forgotten about?

Their plastic problem solved, Boots and Tim got ready to continue their trek. They struggled on through the heat for most of the day. As they reached the top of a sand-dune Tim spotted something.

Look! A camel caravan! Let's catch up with them and see if we can hire some camels.

I wonder who they are.

Desert people
The Tuareg — desert nomads who breed camels, sheep and goats and are famous for guiding camel caravans (No, not that sort of caravan! A.A.) across the desert. The camels carry goods for trading. The men wear long, blue robes and blue, black and white veils across their faces. The veils keep out sand, wind and evil spirits.

Oh no, we'll never catch them up and they're too far away to hear us.

Don't worry. I might be able to get their attention.

How can Boots and Tim signal to the Tuareg?

Eventually, Boots and Tim were able to join the camel caravan. The camel riders were friendlier than Boots and Tim had expected. Unfortunately, they were heading in a different direction, but they invited Boots and Tim to spend the night in their camp.

Aren't you going to help?

In a minute. I'm just trying to find our bearings. If the acacia tree is to the north, the camels must be east of the camp...

Once the camp was set up, it was time to have some fun! The Tuareg invited Boots and Tim to join them for an evening, listening to Tuareg songs and poems, and drinking tea.

Tuareg tents — if you're a Tuareg on the move, you need a home that's quick to put up and quick to pull down. In fact, you need a tent made of camel leather stretched over a wooden frame. Sticks are sometimes stuck around the tent to fend off wild animals.

Before they went to their tent, Boots and Tim bartered for two camels for the next morning.

BARTERING TIPS.
1. Don't accept the first price you're given — it's simply to test the water (so to speak).
2. Cut the price in half and start from there.
3. Work your way upwards in (small) stages.
4. Keep going to the bitter end. It doesn't look good to give in halfway through!
Good luck! (A.A.)

The camel — the perfect desert creature (if a little bad tempered at times, A.A.). Can go for days or months without water. Unbeatable as a means of transport, a beast of burden and provider of milk, meat (for feasts only) and leather (for tents).

Eyelashes — has two sets of long, thick eyelashes to protect eyes from sand, sun and dust.

Hump — stores food in hump, as fat Arabian/African camel has one hump, the Asian camel has two.

Nostrils — can be closed to keep out sand and dust.

Long neck — keeps head above ground where the air is much cooler.

Broad feet — splayed toes act like sandshoes and stop the camel sinking in the sand.

Never try to outspit a camel — you'll lose!

The bartering over, Boots and Tim went to see their new companions. But while they were checking the camels, a sandstorm suddenly blew up!

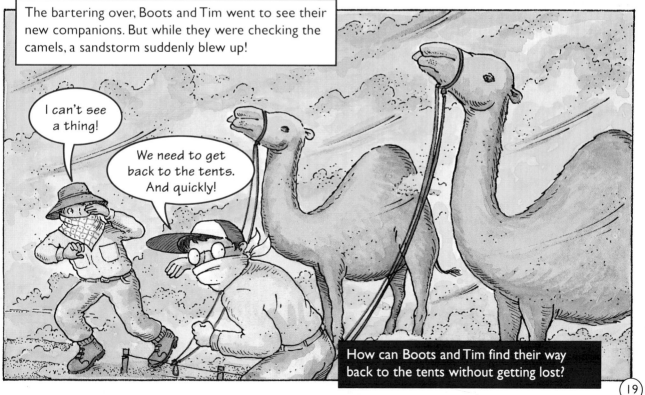

I can't see a thing!

We need to get back to the tents. And quickly!

How can Boots and Tim find their way back to the tents without getting lost?

At midday, they stopped and sheltered by a rock for shade. It was really hot by now. Tim unpacked the present that the Tuareg had given them. It was a pot and glasses for making some tea.

Tuareg tea-making — when you arrive in a Tuareg camp, the first thing you'll be given is a small glass of strong, sweet mint tea. Drink it quickly (don't burn your tongue!) and make lots of nice slurping noises to show you're enjoying it! Three glasses and you know you're welcome and can stay. Four glasses and you're welcome but it's time to go.

After a few failed attempts, Tim managed to brew some tea for Boots and himself.

How far have we come? It feels as though we've been travelling for ages.

I don't know. Let's look at the map.

Can you work out where Boots and Tim are?

After working out their position, Boots and Tim set off again. But Tim still had his nose in Aunt Agatha's diary!

SPOTTER'S GUIDE TO DESERT DWELLERS

Sand grouse — father flies miles to water hole to soak breast feathers in water. Then flies back to nest so chicks can suck the water off. (Fathers, take note! A.A.)

Addax — this very rare antelope never drinks a drop. That's because it gets all the moisture it needs from the plants and seeds it eats.

Desert scorpion — a very nasty sting in the tail. Mainly used for self-defence, not attack. Mainly! Shelters in burrow by day. Hunts at night for beetles and lizards.

Desert locust — not a problem individually, but sometimes forms huge swarms, millions strong, which devastate whole fields. Will eat anything with even a vague vegetable flavour.

Spiny tailed agama — this lizard stores fat in its long, scaly tail for times when food is scarce. One tailful is enough to last a month.

Desert plants — very few plants feel at home in the desert. It's just too hot and dry. Those that do are often scrubby trees or waxy succulents which store water in the leaves. Of course, the most famous desert plant of all — the cactus — does not grow in the Sahara. To see it, you'd need to travel to the American deserts. And that's another journey.

Five plants you might see in the Sahara:

1. Desert melon — DO NOT EAT! It'll make you sick.

2. Oleander — pink flowers (Very pretty A.A.)

3. Date palm

4. Chou Fleur — looks like a rock but is really a plant. (Its name is French for cauliflower! A.A.)

5. Acacia tree — prickly characters

The desert seemed to stretch on for ever, and the oasis village was still nowhere in sight!

Where is this oasis?!

We should reach it soon – at least, I hope so.

Have you got the compass?

It's in my bag! We're headed straight for the oasis – we don't need a compass now.

Don't worry, we're on the right track. I bet they lead to the oasis – we'll just follow them.

But Tim isn't so sure. Can you work out why?

Finally Boots gave in and checked their route with the compass. They were now on the last leg of their journey, or so they hoped. They were certainly on *their* last legs!

Suddenly...

Water! At last.

I don't believe it.

But however far and however fast they walked, they never came any closer to the oasis.

It seems further away than ever!

Then, just as they were about to despair, they saw, in the distance, another three oases with just the same shimmering water. But these were surrounded by palm trees.

The heat's fried my brain – now I can see four of them!

DESERT DIARY

Let's see what A.A. has to say about this.

OK. So all we have to do is head towards the right oasis!

Whichever one that is!

Oasis — a rare haven of greenness and wetness in the desert! A place where underground water comes to the surface. Used as a watering hole for people and animals. Many oases have small towns at their edges because these are the only places in the desert where people can grow crops, eg palm trees (the ones that dates grow on, AA). See Mirage.

Mirage — a trick of the light which can drive a desert traveller mad with thirst. Caused by hot desert air bending the light from a distant (real) oasis so that it looks as if there is a (fake) oasis on the horizon but there isn't. (If you get my drift, AA.) You can never reach it because it doesn't exist. See Oasis.

But which one is it?

On reaching the right oasis, Boots and Tim let out a huge sigh of relief. For, there, on the edge of the oasis stood the very village they were looking for. The one marked on their map with a big X.

We've made it!

Life in an oasis — not all desert people are nomads. Some have settled around oases and built villages and towns. Here there's plenty of water for animals and for growing crops, such as dates. Some larger towns have busy markets where nomads come to buy and sell goods. (A good place to start your bartering! AA.)

But where was Aunt Agatha?

Suddenly, they heard a voice they recognized only too well.

Now, be careful with those. They're 80 million years old, if they're a day!

It was Aunt Agatha, herself. And she had just unearthed her latest, most famous find – a clutch of fossilized dinosaur eggs.

DID YOU SEE?

Did you spot the following creatures in the desert? If not, go back and see if you can find them.

1. desert scorpion

2. jerboa

3. horned viper

4. fennec fox

5. desert hedgehog

6. skink

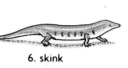

7. sand cat

8. sand grouse

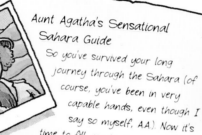

9. spiny-tailed agama

10. Arabian camel

11. desert locust

12. addax antelope

Aunt Agatha's Sensational Sahara Guide

So you've survived your long journey through the Sahara (of course, you've been in very capable hands, even though I say so myself, AA). Now it's time to fill you in on some more stunning Saharan statistics. Here goes...

The sensational Sahara is the world's biggest desert. It covers more than 9,000,000 sq km of north Africa, bounded by the Atlantic Ocean to the west, the Atlas Mountains and Mediterranean Sea to the north, Egypt and the Red Sea to the east, and Sudan and the valley of the Niger River to the south. But thanks to shifting sand-dunes, and overfarming the land, these boundaries are changing year by year. Believe it or not, the Sahara was once lush and green. Millet (a type of grain) was farmed there more than 8,000 years ago. But it's got drier and drier ever since then.

The Sahara can be split into various regions. The Western Sahara (sometimes called the Sahara proper) is an area of rocky plains and sandy "seas". It gets hardly any rain but has several underground rivers which flow from the Atlas and other mountains. These sometimes rise to the surface to provide water for oases where dates and other crops can be grown. The central, mountainous part of the Sahara is some 580-760 metres above sea level, with peaks rising more than 3,000 metres. There's more rain here and some of the peaks are even capped with snow in winter.

The driest part of the Sahara is the Libyan Desert in the east. There's almost no rain and very few oases. The landscape is dominated by sandy wastes and huge sand-dunes, 122 metres or more in height.

However, the whole of the Sahara has a dry climate, with less than 127mm of rain a year. Some places get no rain for years on end. Temperatures range from freezing at night to a scorching 54°C during the day. Except in the oases, hardly any plants can grow, apart from a few thorny shrubs and bushes. At the oases, though, there are date palms a-plenty. (I love dates, don't you? AA) Some artificial oases have also been made by drilling wells more than 1,000 metres deep into the rocky ground. And the northern Sahara has become very important, in recent years, with the discovery of vast amounts of oil.

HOW WOULD YOU SURVIVE IN THE DESERT?

Try this quick quiz to see how well you'd survive in the desert. Then check your survival rating at the end.

1. *Why do the Tuareg wear veils?*

a) to look mysterious
b) to keep out the wind
c) to scare off evil spirits

2. *If you were in an erg, where would you be?*

a) in a rocky desert
b) in a stony desert
c) in a sandy desert

3. *Which plant would you not see in the Sahara?*

a) cactus
b) date palm
c) acacia

4. *What would you do if a djinn caught up with you?*

a) offer it some water
b) cover your eyes, nose and mouth
c) talk to it nicely

5. *Why are so many desert creatures nocturnal?*

a) they're too shy to come out in the day
b) it's cooler to come out at night
c) they don't like bright lights

6. *How long would you survive without water in the desert?*

a) two days
b) two weeks
c) two hours

7. *If a Tuareg offered to teach you tifinagh, what would you learn?*

a) dancing
b) tea-making
c) the Tuareg alphabet

8. *Why are camels called "ships of the desert"?*

a) because they sail over the sand
b) because riding one makes you feel seasick
c) because A.A. says so

9. *Which of these desert creatures is the most poisonous?*

a) horned viper
b) desert scorpion
c) camel

10. *And finally, how do you stop camel milk from going sour?*

a) make it into butter or cheese
b) stop looking at it!
c) add some sugar

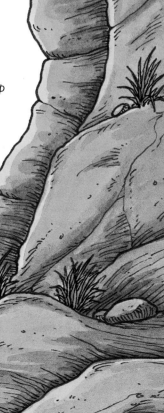

ANSWERS

PAGE 4

Aunt Agatha's message
should say:

I'M IN THE SAHARA DESERT IN NORTH AFRICA (SEE
MAP) AND I'VE JUST MADE AN AMAZING DISCOVERY.
BRING MY CAMERA IMMEDIATELY AND ALL WILL BE
REVEALED. I'M STAYING IN AN OASIS VILLAGE (SEE
X ON MAP).
LOVE AUNT AGATHA
P.S. IF YOU COME ACROSS ANY OF THOSE HEART-
SHAPED SWEETS I LIKE, PLEASE BRING A PACKET.

PAGE 9

The six things they could leave behind are: travel kettle
(they won't be able to plug it anywhere), German
phrasebook (there's not much call for German in the
Sahara), bucket and spade, snorkel and flippers,
dehydrated food (water's too precious) and fishing hook
and line.

PAGE 10

To orientate their map, Boots and Tim should:
1. Lay the map out flat on the ground.
2. Hold the compass above it.
3. Wait for the tip of the compass needle to point north.
4. Turn the map round until the grid lines running north
point in the same direction as the needle.
5. Now head in the opposite direction!

PAGE 11

PAGE 12

PAGE 13

Boots and Tim are at grid reference 5D on the map. The
safest place for them to sleep is in the cave high up above
the wadi (to avoid unwelcome visitors and flash floods).

PAGE 15

The jerboa was the intruder. (Its tail is peeking out from behind Boots' backpack and you can see prints of its long back legs in the sand.) The disaster awaiting them when they wake up is that Boots' water bottle has been knocked over and all the water has poured out.

PAGE 16

Tim has forgotten the black plastic bin bag (see Essential Survival Kit on page 8).

PAGE 17

Boots and Tim could signal to the Tuareg using their mirror to catch the sun's rays and flash them in the Tuareg's direction. (NB Be careful not to look directly at the sun, or the reflection in the mirror – you could do serious damage to the naked eye.)

PAGE 19

Boots and Tim still have their compass with them. If they can remember that the camels are tethered due east of the camp, they can use the compass to find a westward route back to the Tuareg camp.

PAGE 20

Tim could use the blow-up cushion to make his camel ride more comfortable.

PAGE 21

Boots and Tim have reached grid reference 8E on the map.

PAGE 23

They are actually following their own footprints. If you spotted the patterns on the soles of their shoes on page 21, you'll see that they match the footprints Boots and Tim are following. (You might also spot the cup that Tim dropped earlier.)

PAGE 25

The right oasis is at grid reference 9F on the map. It's the oasis you can see in the top right of the page. Boots and Tim can work this out by comparing the landmarks they can see with those marked on the map.

PAGE 27

Aunt Agatha's camera is around the neck of Boots' camel. Boots put it there for safe-keeping when they stopped for tea and a rest on page 21. At the same time, Tim's camel was tucking into A.A.'s heart-shaped sweets.

HOW WOULD YOU SURVIVE...

ANSWERS

1. b) and **c)** Tuareg men wear veils wrapped round their heads to protect them from the wind *and* from evil spirits that lurk in the desert. These veils can be blue, black or white. The blue veils are called *tagilmusts*, and the Tuareg refer to themselves as *Kel Tagilmust*, or "people of the veil". Women wear much smaller veils, covering their mouths.

2. c) *Erg* is the Arabic name for sandy desert and for the great "seas" of sand and sand-dunes which cover parts of the Sahara. *Reg* is the name for a stony desert. Patches of rocky desert are called *hammada*.

3. a) If you see a cactus (even a small one), you're in the wrong desert! Cacti only grow in the American deserts. Deserts are found in many parts of the world – Africa, Asia, Australia, the Middle East and North and South America. Strictly speaking, even the icy wastes of Antarctica officially count as desert. (But that's another adventure, A.A.)

4. b) A *djinn* is a dust devil, a particularly small and violent type of dust storm. They just seem to spring up from nowhere, especially in the afternoons. (My advice is to cover your nose and mouth with a damp hanky to stop the dust choking you. Speaking to it nicely will do no good whatsoever! A.A.) Unbelievably, the Sahara Desert produces between 60-200 million tonnes of dust a year. That's an awful lot of dust!

5. b) You might think it's a good idea to travel by day and sleep by night, but most desert creatures have more sense. Many spend the day underground where the temperature can be a pleasant 30°C cooler than on the surface. They wake up at dusk and leave their shelters to hunt for food.

6. a) You could survive for days without food, but after just two days without water, you'd be dead. An adult human being could lose up to nine litres of water on an active day in the desert. You face two major problems in the desert –
1) you can lose a litre of water an hour in sweat
2) there's not much water about to replace it.

7. c) The *tifinagh* is the name of the ancient Tuareg alphabet. It used to be made up of consonants only and was used only for more general communication and for literature. The Tuareg have a rich tradition of songs and poetry.

8. b) Camels walk with a rather peculiar, swaying motion which can make you feel slightly seasick until you get used to it. (And if you don't believe me, try it for yourself! A.A.)

9. a) and **b)** Horned vipers are among the most poisonous snakes in the desert. Trouble is, they're so tricky to see. They lie under the sand, camouflaged, with just their two "horns" poking out. If a juicy jerboa hops by, they strike... Desert scorpions are also extremely poisonous, with a nasty sting in their tails. (Camels are not poisonous, though they do tend to spit! A.A.)

10. a) Some desert people put salt in camel milk to stop it going sour in the heat or they make it into butter or cheese. They do the same thing with sheep and goat milk.

SO HOW DID YOU DO?

8-10	Well done! A Tuareg in the making!
4-7	Quite good but you need to read my diary again.
1-3	Better luck next time. If there is a next time. At this rate, you won't survive very long!

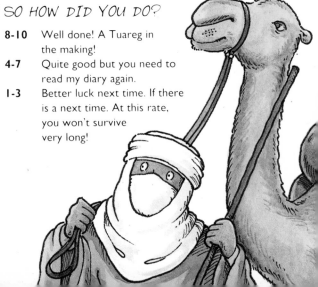